j921 Fremont
Souza, D. M. (Dorothy M.)
John C. Fremont

D1604828

John C. Frémont

John C. Frémont

D. M. Souza

Franklin Watts
A Division of Scholastic Inc.
New York • Toronto • London • Auckland • Sydney
Mexico City • New Delhi • Hong Kong
Danbury, Connecticut

Note to readers: Definitions for words in **bold** can be found in the Glossary at the back of this book.

Photographs © 2004: Art Resource, NY/National Portrait Gallery, Smithsonian Institution: 31; Bancroft Library, University of California, Berkeley: 30, 34, 50; Bridgeman Art Library International Ltd., London/New York: 11 (The Stapleton Collection), 17 (New York Historical Society), 48 (Brooklyn Museum of Art, New York, USA); Brigham Young University, Provo, UT, L. Tom Perry Special Collections, Harold B. Lee Library: 2, 18, 20, 22, 25, 27, 44, 46; College of Charleston Libraries, Special Collections: 9; Corbis Images: 40 (Gerald French), 42 (Pete Saloutos); Hulton|Archive/Getty Images: 35; National Archives and Records Administration: 19; National Geographic Image Collection/James L. Amos: 26; National Postal Museum/Smithsonian Institution: 21; North Wind Picture Archives: 12, 14, 32, 37; Stock Montage, Inc.: 36; The Image Works: 29 (Joe Sohm), 6, 7 (Michael Wickes); Union League Club of Chicago: 13.

The illustration on the cover shows John C. Frémont. The photograph opposite the title page shows Frémont and his expedition navigating treacherous waters.

Library of Congress Cataloging-in-Publication Data

Souza, D. M. (Dorothy M.)
    John C. Frémont / by D. M. Souza.
        p. cm. — (Watts library)
    Summary: Discusses the life and work of John C. Frémont, an explorer of the American West. Includes bibliographical references and index.
    ISBN 0-531-12288-3 (lib. bdg.)   0-531-16652-X (pbk.)
1. Frémont, John Charles, 1813–1890—Juvenile literature. 2. Explorers—West (U.S.)—Biography—Juvenile literature. 3. Explorers—United States—Biography—Juvenile literature. 4. West (U.S.)—Discovery and exploration—Juvenile literature. 5. Presidential candidates—United States—Biography—Juvenile literature. 6. Generals—United States—Biography—Juvenile literature. [1. Frémont, John Charles, 1813–1890. 2. Explorers. 3. West (U.S.)—Discovery and exploration.] I. Title. II. Series.
E415.9.F8S68 2004
979'.02'092—dc22

        2003013347

Contents

Frémont's expeditions helped to encourage people to emigrate to the West.

Chapter One

Young Adventurer

For years the region west of the Mississippi was a vast stretch of land marked by dangers and uncertainties. It was known only to American Indians, fur traders, and rugged bands of settlers seeking a new life. In 1804–1806, Meriwether Lewis and William Clark traveled to the source of the Missouri River, crossed the Rockies, and followed the Columbia River to the Pacific Ocean. Along the way the two men described the rugged beauty and rich natural resources of the land. But not until after the explorations of John Charles Frémont were large numbers of people inspired to move westward.

Frémont not only brought back maps of important places, but named and described rivers and landmarks along the way. He noted the kinds of plants and animals likely to be found, listed supplies and equipment needed to make the journey, and indicated ways of dealing with various Indian peoples. In his colorful reports, written for the government and later released to the public, Frémont painted a picture of a land ripe for settlement—one simply waiting for anyone willing to face the challenges.

Although controversy surrounded much of Frémont's later life, his early expeditions brought him fame. Called "the Pathfinder" by fans of his reports, he encouraged others to follow the trails he marked. His adventures are an important part of frontier history.

Early Years

John Charles Frémont was born on January 21, 1813, in Savannah, Georgia. Five years later, after the births of a brother and sister, his father died and the family moved to Charleston, South Carolina. Here Frémont attended school. At age sixteen, he enrolled at Charleston College where he became fascinated with books on travel. When he was expelled for "irregularity," he decided to leave home and explore new places. Skilled in mathematics, he obtained a job on board the warship *Natchez* and for two years sailed the coast of South

Ghost Writer

Frémont dictated his reports to his wife, Jessie, whom some historians believe frequently added the details that made them both exciting and appealing to the public.

This illustration shows Charleston College around the time that Frémont attended the school.

America teaching mathematics and exchanging ideas with young officers on board. In his spare moments, he studied maps, the constellations, and learned to calculate **latitude** and **longitude**. As he later wrote in his journals, his time at sea "passed too quickly."

Frémont's next position was with the Corps of Topographical Engineers, a branch of the army that explored and mapped wilderness areas. Loving nature, he worked for a summer as an assistant **surveyor** of a proposed railroad route from Charleston to Cincinnati. To him the job was a "kind of picnic with work enough to give it zest."

In 1836, in response to white settlers' desire to farm Cherokee lands in North Carolina, Tennessee, and Georgia, the corps sent a survey party, including Frémont, to map the area. The young adventurer made valuable contacts during this time and learned how to survive in the wilderness. After the experience he decided that the life of an explorer suited him perfectly.

Frémont's reputation as a knowledgeable surveyor quickly spread. When the French geographer and scientist Joseph Nicollet needed a strong young assistant on a journey into the northern territory between the Mississippi and Missouri Rivers, he contacted the young lieutenant. Frémont wasted no time in accepting the job, knowing he could learn many things from this first-rate scientist and explorer.

Under Nicollet's guidance, Frémont mastered the art of studying the stars, observing plants, soils, and minerals, and of making careful sketches of everything he saw. He took part in bison hunts, watched how exchanges were made with American Indians and met a number of **mountain men**, Indian scouts and fur traders, who would prove helpful on his later adventures. When the expedition ended, Frémont was no longer Nicollet's assistant but an experienced explorer.

A Second Home

Once back in Washington, Frémont and Nicollet reported their findings to President Martin Van Buren. In special offices in the city, they spent long hours turning their field notes into official reports. In the evenings they attended dinner parties with scientists, congressmen, and other distinguished guests.

One influential person whom Frémont met while in Washington was the powerful senior senator from Missouri, Thomas Hart Benton. The Benton residence became a second home for him. Dinner conversations there often centered on

Salary

Frémont's pay with Nicollet was four dollars a day. He was also given an expense allowance of ten cents a mile while traveling to St. Louis to meet the explorer.

extending the nation's borders to the Pacific. The senator and many of his friends felt that land was needed for the nation's growing population. However, Great Britain's foothold in the Pacific Northwest and its close relations with Mexico was seen as a threat. Benton was convinced that acquiring land—even if it meant going to war with other nations—was necessary for survival. Because of this he and others strongly supported **Manifest Destiny**, the idea that the United States was destined to extend its borders from coast to coast. It did not take Frémont long to also become an enthusiastic **expansionist**.

During this time Frémont met and fell in love with Jessie Benton, one of the senator's daughters. Her parents were not

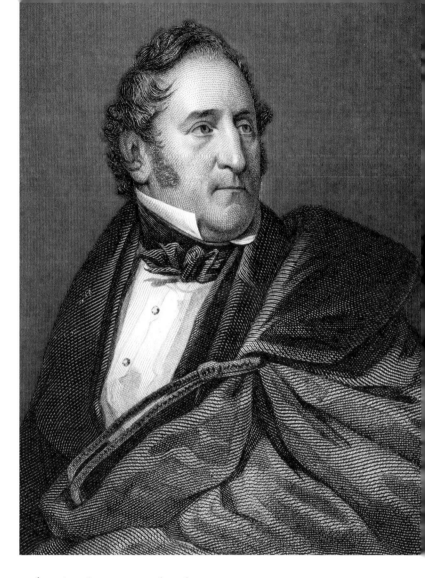

Thomas Hart Benton served as a U.S. senator and a representative during his career.

The Senator from Missouri

Thomas Benton was born in North Carolina but later moved to Missouri. When that state was admitted to the Union, he became its first senator and served in Congress for thirty years.

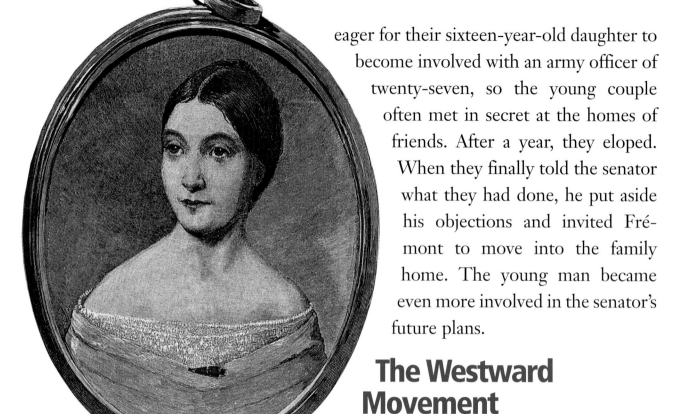

Jessie was a great help to her husband and later in her life she wrote books about her experiences.

eager for their sixteen-year-old daughter to become involved with an army officer of twenty-seven, so the young couple often met in secret at the homes of friends. After a year, they eloped. When they finally told the senator what they had done, he put aside his objections and invited Frémont to move into the family home. The young man became even more involved in the senator's future plans.

The Westward Movement

In Congress, Benton, or one of his friends, repeatedly tried introducing bills that would grant settlers western lands or guarantee them protection. Each time the bills failed to pass—mainly because the new president, John Tyler, opposed any idea of expansion. The president was afraid that a government-sponsored westward movement might cause trouble with Great Britain. As a result, the senator realized he had to try another approach.

Knowing that an expedition led by the Topographical Corps would not arouse Tyler's suspicions, Benton began seeking help for the project. If the government did not recognize the need for western expansion, he did. And the most

12

Frémont prepared for an exciting but difficult journey to explore the West.

qualified person to lead such an expedition was his son-in-law, John Charles Frémont.

Once arrangements were made with the corps, Frémont received his orders to head to Fort Leavenworth and survey the Platte River in present-day Nebraska. If time permitted, he was also to survey the Kansas River. Prompted by Senator Benton, he would eventually map the Oregon Trail as far as South Pass in the Wind River Mountains of Wyoming.

Charles Preuss accompanied Frémont on several expeditions.

Chapter Two

Journey to South Pass

During preparations for the expedition in late 1841, Frémont met and hired Charles Preuss, a skilled German **cartographer**, or mapmaker, who would accompany him on several expeditions. He then traveled to New York to buy scientific instruments. Among his purchases was a rubber boat, 20 feet (6 m) long and 5 feet (1.5 meters) wide with, as he described it, "air-tight compartments, to be used in crossing or examining water

Secret Journal

Charles Preuss later proved to be moody and often depressed. On the journey he kept a diary in German in which he repeatedly complained about Frémont and about the hardships and dangers of the expedition.

courses." He also bought an instrument for taking photographs called **daguerreotypes**.

Senator Benton believed that Jessie's twelve-year-old brother Randolph could profit from the wilderness experience, so he arranged for the boy to be part of the expedition. Randolph's nineteen-year-old cousin, Henry Brant, would also join them in St. Louis. Frémont welcomed both on what would be an exciting adventure.

St. Louis and Beyond

In early May 1842, Frémont and Randolph said goodbye to Jessie, who was three months pregnant, and left by carriage for the Washington railway station. Three weeks later, they arrived in St. Louis where Frémont checked and rechecked supplies. He hired twenty-one men, all of whom had worked in the wilderness as fur traders.

On June 10, eight members of the expedition traveled overland with the horses, mules, oxen and eight carts loaded with supplies. The others left by steamboat with Frémont. Both groups were to meet at a trading post at the mouth of the Kansas River.

Frémont knew that a knowledgeable guide was essential for the success of his expedition. Fortunately, Kit Carson, a well-known mountain man, was on board the steamboat and Frémont convinced him to join them. Carson had worked as a trapper, scout, and Indian agent and had a reputation for courage and almost superhuman skills. He was exactly the

Red River Carts

Named after a north-central river, the carts were drawn by oxen and had spoked wheels about 5 feet (1.5 m) in diameter.

person Frémont needed. After everyone arrived at the trading post, the expedition set off on the journey into the wilderness.

Many explorers of the American West, including Lewis and Clark, used St. Louis as the starting point for their expeditions.

A Close Call

In the beginning the routine was the same. The men usually rose at dawn for breakfast. The animals were turned loose to graze for a time and then the group resumed its journey. At noon everyone would stop for one or two hours to eat and rest and then continue the march until sundown.

In a short time the expedition arrived at the place where Frémont had planned to cross the Kansas River. The waterway was about 230 yards (210 m) wide, and spring rains and runoff from snowpacks had turned it into a roaring, swirling, yellow current. The animals became terrified.

The men managed to lead the horses across, but they left the oxen, carts and supplies on the other side. The next morning Frémont's rubber boat was put to the test. Wheels, body, and supplies from one cart were disassembled and loaded onto

17

Members of Frémont's expedition break camp and prepare to continue on with their journey.

Wildlife

Wolves, elk, antelope, deer, bison, and flocks of turkeys were common sights, and some were killed for food. At one point Frémont wrote "as we were riding quietly along the bank, a grand herd of buffalo, some seven or eight hundred in number, came crowding up from the river...and the distance across the prairie (two or three miles) gave us fine opportunity to charge them before they could get among the river hills."

the craft. Three men attempted to paddle across the river but had trouble keeping the vessel from drifting downstream. Basil Lajeunesse, a powerful swimmer, jumped into the water, grabbed the boat's line, put it between his teeth and swam to the other side where the rest of the men helped pull it ashore.

Several more trips were made in the same way, but as nightfall approached, two carts still had to be moved. Frémont ordered the men to load these and their supplies onto the boat. As the vessel moved across the water, waves broke over the side and the **helmsman** panicked. The next instant, the boat capsized and carts, barrels, boxes, and guns were swept away in the current. All the men jumped into the icy water. They were able to save almost everything except some sugar and a large bag containing the journey's entire supply of coffee. Everyone was exhausted from the ordeal and provisions were waterlogged. The next morning Frémont declared the day one of rest and relaxation.

While the men were encamped, several Indians arrived.

One spoke French and Frémont **bartered** with him for about 30 pounds (14 kilograms) of coffee and other supplies. That night the men ate well and were ready for their next day's march.

The Unexpected

Thunder, lightning, and torrential rains were common on the journey, as were swarms of mosquitoes. Still, the expedition moved on. Most days, they advanced about 24 miles (39 kilometers). Each evening while everyone slept, Frémont worked in his tent recording the events of the day, latitude and longitude, temperatures, and descriptions of the plants and animals they had seen.

On July 5, the party split into two groups. Twenty-five members, guided by Kit Carson, followed the North Fork of the Platte River. A smaller group went with Frémont along the South Fork to a trading post where they hoped to find fresh mules. Both groups planned to reunite at Fort Laramie, another trading post, in present-day Wyoming.

Four days into their journey, Frémont and his followers spotted a number of warriors charging in their direction. As they prepared to defend

This is a page from Frémont's report on the first expedition.

I stood on a narrow crest, about three feet in width, with an inclination of about 20°, north 51°E. As soon as I had gratified the first feelings of curiosity, I descended and each man ascended in his turn, for I would only allow one at a time to mount the unstable and precarious slab, which it seemed a breath would hurl into the abyss below. We mounted the barometer in the snow of the summit, and fixing a ram rod in a crevice, unfurled the national flag, to wave in the breeze where never flag waved before. During our morning's ascent we had met no sign of animal life, except the small sparrow like bird

Fort Laramie was started in the 1830s by fur traders.

themselves, one of the men in the expedition recognized the Indians as the Arapahos with whom he had once lived. Quickly he called to their leader and the attack was halted. That evening Frémont and his men were invited to a feast in the Indians' village.

Meanwhile, Carson met a band of fur trappers headed by his old friend Jim Bridger. Both groups camped together for the night and Randolph and Henry were held spellbound by the wild stories the mountain men told. Before leaving, Bridger warned that the number of "whites" entering the area was angering the Sioux, and it would be dangerous for the party to travel any farther. In spite of this, Carson and his group headed out and in two days reached the base of Chimney Rock in present-day Nebraska.

With two fresh horses and three mules, Frémont and his party crossed barren, parched lands where temperatures

Career of Bridger

Only seventeen when he became a member of the Jedediah Smith expedition into the Upper Missouri, Jim Bridger was the first white man to see the Great Salt Lake. His path across the Rockies (Bridger Pass) later became the route for overland mail, the Union Pacific Railroad, and eventually for Interstate 80.

reached more than 100 degrees Fahrenheit (38 degrees Celsius). They arrived at Laramie and heard from their companions about the **hostile** Sioux. Frémont made arrangements for Randolph and Henry to remain behind at the fort, and he and the rest of the expedition headed west.

The Final Push

Goat Island, Independence Rock, and Devil's Gate were a few of the places Frémont noted next in his journal. On August 8 the party reached South Pass and were captivated by the sight of the snow-peaked mountains surrounding them. Frémont was determined to explore the area even farther.

The next day, although running short of food, he had some of his men fell several trees and build a kind of fort for protection. Then he took a party of fourteen to scale the highest peak. The climb was difficult and several men and animals had to be left behind. Finally, with five others, Frémont reached what he described as "a nearly perpendicular wall of granite." Standing on top, where no explorer had stood, he fixed a rod in a crevice and unfurled the American flag. According to his notes, the elevation was 13,570 feet (4,125 m).

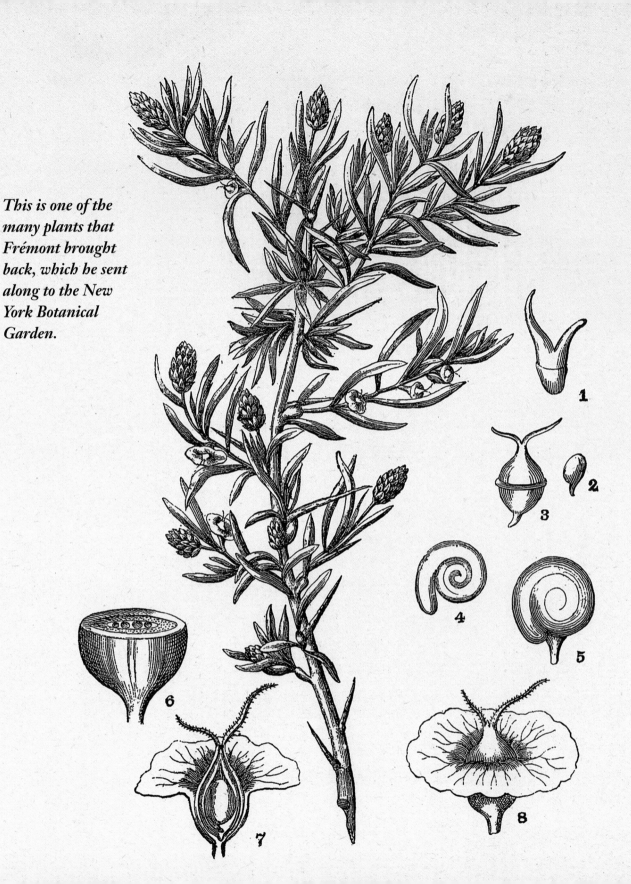

This is one of the many plants that Frémont brought back, which he sent along to the New York Botanical Garden.

Chapter Three

Beyond the Rockies

Everyone at the Benton household was relieved when word arrived that the members of the first expedition had safely reached St. Louis. On October 29, 1842, Frémont and Randolph returned home. They was just in time. Jessie was about to give birth to a daughter.

Frémont still had several tasks to complete. He was responsible for sending plants collected on the expedition to the New York Botanical Garden. He also had to rework maps and rewrite journal notes in the form of an official report.

The book-length report was published in March of the following year. One senator suggested that a thousand copies be printed for the general public. Soon people were talking about Frémont, the Pathfinder. Senator Benton immediately began making arrangements for another westward expedition to be led by his now famous son-in-law.

Secret Plans

Before the month ended, Frémont was assigned to lead a second expedition beyond the Rockies. He was to attempt to complete a survey of the Northwest that was begun earlier by a naval commander. But on the return trip Benton urged him to travel east by way of the Oregon Trail to locate the best sites for future military forts.

Thirty-nine men signed on for this expedition—among them Charles Preuss, from the first expedition, Jacob Dodson, an eighteen-year-old free black who worked for the senator, Thomas "Broken Hand" Fitzpatrick, a legendary mountain

Oregon Trail

Stretching from Independence, Missouri, to the Columbia River in Oregon, this 2,000-mile (3,219-km) trail was rugged, poorly marked, and very dangerous in places.

"Broken Hand"

Born in Ireland, Thomas Fitzpatrick ran away from home at the age of seventeen and became a sailor. After joining an expedition to find the source of the Missouri River, he worked as a scout and trapper. One day a musket exploded in his left hand and blew off two fingers. Indians then gave him the nickname of "Broken Hand, Chief of all mountain men."

man who served as guide, and two Delaware Indians. Twelve carts, each drawn by two mules, carried all the supplies, and a light covered wagon held Frémont's scientific equipment. A **howitzer,** or small cannon, which Frémont felt would offer protection against warring Indians, was also loaded onto a small wagon.

When word leaked about the cannon, Frémont's superiors ordered him to return to Washington and explain why he was taking such a weapon on a scientific expedition. Jessie received the message first. Not wishing to see her husband delayed, she sent another message urging him to leave immediately.

This illustration shows the second expedition near the Snake River. The howitzer is in the foreground.

Crossing the Great Basin

Frémont and his party quickly left St. Louis on May 13, 1843, and moved along the Kansas River. After advancing some distance, the Pathfinder decided to detour south with some of his men. Twenty-five others were left under the leadership of Broken Hand. Eventually the two groups would meet at Fort Hall in present-day Idaho.

At a campsite below the settlement of Pueblo, Colorado, Kit Carson joined the expedition's leader as he and his small

Part of the Oregon Trail ran across the Great Basin.

party made their way slowly toward the Great Salt Lake. Frémont was the first to use the term Great Basin to describe the land extending from the Wasatch Mountains in Utah and Idaho to the Sierra Nevada mountains in California. His maps of the basin later encouraged Brigham Young to establish a Mormon settlement in the region.

Frémont and his men endured many hardships. When rations were low, they were forced to eat stewed skunk, roots,

Frémont Island

Frémont and his companions took the rubber boat out to an island in the middle of the Great Salt Lake. There is a cross on a rock that some believe Carson carved. It can still be seen today.

and bitter wild cherries. They continued in spite of temperature extremes and threats from hostile Indians who worried that the increasing number of "whites" on their lands was a sign of more dangerous invasions to come.

Finally, in August, the two groups met as scheduled near Fort Hall, a British post. Frémont felt that the next leg of their journey would be even more difficult and dismissed eleven men who were eager to return to St. Louis. After resting for several days and renewing supplies, members of the expedition set off again.

They passed impressive falls, lava boulders, sagebrush, and snowcapped mountains. By early October they reached Fort Boise, a Hudson's Bay Company trading post. Almost two months later they arrived at The Dalles in Oregon where the main party encamped. Frémont, Preuss, and two others went by canoe down the Columbia River as far as Fort Vancouver, the

This illustration shows the Frémont expedition riding rapids on the Columbia River.

Hudson's Bay Headquarters

Fort Vancouver was named after the British navigator, George Vancouver, who first explored the Pacific Northwest between 1792 and 1794. Its trading post contained storehouses, a bakery, carpenter shop, a blacksmith shop where knives, axes, traps were made and sold to anyone in need. It even had a jail.

Hudson's Bay Company headquarters. Here they completed the expedition's official assignment.

While at Fort Vancouver, Frémont saw American **emigrants** arriving daily to buy needed supplies and obtain information. As he noted in his journal, "this friendly assistance was of very great value to the emigrants, whose families were otherwise exposed to much suffering." After resting for several days, he purchased provisions for the three-month return trip. Then he and his companions left the fort to join the others encamped at The Dalles.

A Dangerous Detour

By the time Frémont reached The Dalles, everything was ready for the expedition's departure. Carts had been sold, supplies, except for the howitzer and its wagon, were loaded onto horses and mules, and excitement was high. Frémont was not planning to return by the same route he had come. Even though winter was approaching, he wanted to explore more of the Great Basin and try to discover the location of a body of water that supposedly led to the Pacific Ocean.

Moving along the Cascade Range, the expedition pushed toward what is now Reno, Nevada. Trekking through snow and frozen streams and across jagged rocks took its toll on the men and animals. When rations were low, they managed to obtain salmon and pine nuts from various Indian tribes.

Finally, the poor condition of the animals and lack of food prompted Frémont to turn west again. According to Carson,

New Helvetia

Born in Baden, Germany, John Sutter lived most of his life in the United States. For three years, he worked as a trader in Missouri and then headed west. In 1841, he was able to secure from the Mexican government a large tract of land where he established a trading post in New Helvetia, a settlement near the present-day city of Sacramento. New Helvetia later became known as Sutter's Fort.

if they crossed the Sierra Nevada range and entered the Sacramento Valley, they would find supplies in the settlement of Captain Sutter. The men were enthusiastic at the thought of reaching civilization again and having a good meal. Even though a number of the region's Indians tried discouraging them from crossing the mountains during winter, they began their ascent.

As the men climbed higher, deep snow, biting winds, and hunger made progress difficult. The howitzer had to be abandoned as well as several mules and horses. At one point Frémont described their situation in these words, "the times were severe when stout men lost their minds from extremity of suffering—when mules and horses, ready to die of starvation were killed for food."

The Cascade Range is part of the Sierra Nevada mountain range.

At Sutter's settlement, the expedition was able to get some much needed rest.

Finally, on March 8, the expedition reached Sutter's settlement. The men needed time to rest and remained there for more than two weeks. When they moved out, they had 130 fresh horses and mules, 30 head of cattle, and packs full of supplies. An Indian boy from the fort was assigned to serve as their guide.

The Return

By mid-April 1844, the expedition had traveled more than 500 miles (805 km), before rounding the southern part of the Sierra Nevada mountains and turning northeast. Despite the constant threat of horse thieves, they finally reached Pueblo on June 28. Almost a month later, having traveled more than 3,500 miles (5,633 km), they arrived in Kansas on the Missouri River.

For his accomplishments, Frémont was made a captain in the army. He and Jessie eagerly began preparing the report of his expedition for publication. When the document was released to the public, Frémont was again hailed as a hero. It did not take long for him to grow tired of the social and political scene and ask to be sent on another mission.

The report of Frémont's second expedition was well received and garnered Frémont a lot of attention.

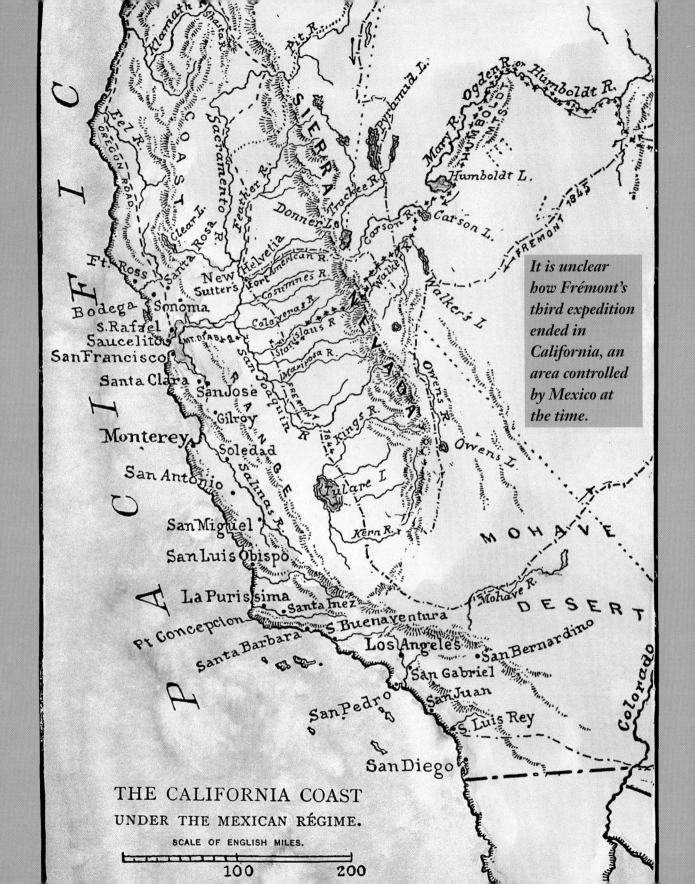

It is unclear how Frémont's third expedition ended in California, an area controlled by Mexico at the time.

THE CALIFORNIA COAST

UNDER THE MEXICAN RÉGIME.

SCALE OF ENGLISH MILES.

100   200

Chapter Four

Trouble in California

Frémont's third expedition, which left Kansas City in late June of 1845, was unique. Not only did events change the course of his career, but they also altered the boundaries of the nation. Although directed by his superiors to survey the territory around Bent's Fort—in present-day Colorado—and to return by December 1845, he followed neither of these orders. It is not known whether Senator Benton or someone else gave him other instructions. But, for some reason, Frémont ended up in a battle for Mexican-controlled Alta California.

For a number of years, more and more settlers had been entering California. To many of them, the area seemed like a foreign land, one that they hoped would some day be taken over by the United States government. Meanwhile Pio Pico, the Mexican governor in Los Angeles, and General José Castro, the commandant in Monterey, struggled to keep the territory and its inhabitants under Mexico's control.

General José Castro did not want Frémont and his expedition to stay in the area for too long.

A Stand in Monterey

Soon after reaching Sutter's Fort in December, Frémont took eight of his men south to Monterey. Not wishing the armed expedition of sixty men to alarm the Mexicans, he first met with Thomas Larkin, the American **consul,** and then with Castro. He assured both that he was in California to rest his men and animals and to purchase supplies for an expedition to Oregon. Castro reluctantly gave him permission to stay until he obtained what he needed.

Two months later, when Castro learned that Frémont and his party were still in the area, he sent a message demanding their immediate withdrawal. Instead of obeying, Frémont ordered his men to the top of nearby Hawk's Peak (now Frémont's Peak). There they built a makeshift fort, and raised the American flag. Castro called for volunteers to drive out the intruders.

In the middle of the night, before a shot had been fired, Frémont for some reason led his men down the other side of the mountain and headed north. This made Castro furious and he issued an order to drive out all foreigners. Groups of settlers suddenly began uniting to resist attacks.

Threat of War

Meanwhile Archibald Gillespie, a young lieutenant from Washington, arrived by ship in Monterey Bay with two messages from James Buchanan, the secretary of state. One message was for Thomas Larkin and the other was for Frémont. We do not know the contents of Frémont's letter. All we know

Frémont meets with Archibald Gillespie who brought him orders from Buchanan.

Bear Flag Revolt

Although Frémont did not take part in their struggle, he did advise a group of settlers who were resisting Castro's soldiers. Calling themselves Osos, the Spanish word for "bears," they captured the town of Sonoma on June 14, 1846, forced the surrender of General Vallejo, and raised a flag depicting a grizzly bear, a symbol of the Republic of California.

is that after reading it, Frémont wrote in his journal that he felt relieved of his duty as an explorer and would now act as "an officer of the American Army." The threat of war was obviously in the air.

In July, as soon as Frémont heard that a United States naval force under Commodore Robert F. Stockton had raised the American flag over Monterey, he returned to that city to offer his assistance. Stockton authorized him to form a "Naval Battalion of Mounted Volunteer Riflemen," and Frémont enlisted almost five hundred men who helped capture both San Juan Bautista and San Jose.

From Monterey, Frémont and some in his command then headed south to San Diego where, with Commodore

Frémont rode with his troops to join Commodore Stockton in San Diego.

Stockton, they raised the American flag without firing a shot. Triumphantly the two men entered Los Angeles. After being convinced that California had been conquered, they returned north.

Power Play

The Mexicans had no intention of surrendering without a fight. When Stockton received word of a revolt in Los Angeles, he asked Frémont to reoccupy the city. Frémont headed overland with one hundred men. At the same time, Brigadier General Stephen Watts Kearny of the U.S. Army was marching toward the city from the south.

On January 13, 1847, the commander of the Mexican forces surrendered to Frémont and signed a treaty ending the fighting in California. The surrender was followed by confusion over who was in command. Was it Kearny, Frémont, or Stockton? Three days later Stockton sailed for the East Coast and named Frémont as California's governor. Kearny angrily withdrew to Monterey and assumed the role of military commander of California.

Repeatedly Frémont refused to recognize Kearny's

Defeat at San Pasqual

Kearny had come west through Santa Fe and at San Pasqual, near San Diego, had been defeated by the Mexicans. By the time he arrived in Los Angeles, he was sick and humiliated by defeat.

authority. This angered Kearny who had been given his command by the army. He began making plans for a **court-martial**. When Frémont finally arrived in Monterey, Kearny stripped him of his authority and ordered him to return east.

In November 1847, Frémont was forced to stand trial for **mutiny**. After eighty-nine days, a panel of officers handed down a verdict of guilty. In February Frémont resigned from the army. In his writings, he never again mentioned either his trial or Kearny.

A Pardon

President James Polk, not satisfied that there was enough evidence to prove that Frémont had committed mutiny, pardoned him and offered to again make him a lieutenant colonel. Frémont refused.

Frémont's report on his third expedition told the Senate about the rich agricultural lands of California.

Chapter Five

Private Expeditions

After his court-martial, Frémont, with the help of Jessie, began writing a report of his third expedition. In 1848, a fifty-page U.S. Senate document was released to the public. In it, California was described as "the Italy of America," a land of plenty where figs, peaches, and grapes grew in abundance. Settlers were more eager than ever to go west, especially once gold was discovered near Sutter's Fort.

The Frémont family next made plans to leave the East Coast and move to a large tract of land in California that had been purchased for them. While a corral, barn and house were being built, Frémont agreed to lead a fourth expedition. Unfortunately it would end in tragedy.

Winter in the San Juans

Backed by Senator Benton and three St. Louis merchants, Frémont was to survey a route for a railroad through the southern Rockies and determine which passes could be used in winter. Unable to obtain government funding, he persuaded those in the expedition to serve without pay until funds could be raised. Thirty-five men agreed to the terms, among them

The southern Rocky Mountains posed a great obstacle to Frémont and his team.

Charles Preuss and fifteen others who had been members of previous expeditions.

The party left St. Louis on October 3, 1848. Early snow and frosts made it clear that winter was going to be especially severe. The men reached Bent's Fort in the middle of November and rested for three days. Although two mountain men advised against moving across the southern Rockies at this time, Frémont refused to turn back.

At Pueblo he hired William Sherley "Old Bill" Williams as a guide. The men then followed the Rio Grande River until they reached the San Juan Range with its towering peaks. Because of the heavy snows on the mountaintops, Williams turned away from the river at the wrong site. This mistake led the expedition across rugged terrain more than 12,000 feet (3,660 m) high.

Deep snows, biting cold, and frequent blizzards forced the men to keep moving or risk being buried alive. Eventually ten men died and 130 pack animals froze to death. When Frémont and some in the party finally reached Taos on January 21, 1849, they were hollow-eyed, ragged and exhausted.

Bad weather and cold climate caused great hardships for Frémont's expedition.

Supplies were quickly sent back to the remainder of the expedition still stranded in the mountains.

A number of the men kept journals that criticized Frémont

and his leadership. Others had only praise for him. In his letters to Jessie, the explorer blamed Williams for the tragic losses of his fourth expedition. Regardless of who was to blame, Frémont remained popular, and after California became a state, he was named one of its first senators.

The Fifth Expedition

The American public continued to call for a **transcontinental** railroad to link the east with the west. In response, Congress authorized $150,000 to survey five possible routes. Senator Benton believed that a central route through the Rockies would be the most valuable and that Frémont would be the best one to survey it. The government, however, chose Captain John Williams Guinnison. Frustrated, Benton and Frémont raised private funds for an expedition.

In September 1853, Frémont recruited twenty-two men. One was Solomon Nunes Carvalho, a painter and photographer. His account would become a major source of information about Frémont's final expedition.

After the men began moving across Kansas, a prairie fire broke out. Only by racing 15 miles (24 km) on horseback through the tall blazing grass were they able to escape. They reached Bent's Fort by the middle of November and rested for a week.

Hoping to cross the mountain passes before the heavy snows fell, they all traveled lightly. Frequently, Frémont was able to follow the wagon ruts left by those on the earlier

The Fatal Expedition

Captain Gunnison and six of his men were later slain by Paiute Indians in Utah.

During his fifth expedition, Frémont had to flee from a prairie fire.

government-sponsored expedition. Indians in the area were at war with one another and the men had to guard constantly against warring parties.

At one point the expedition's lead mule plunged into a deep chasm pulling fifty other mules with it. From then on many of the men were forced to travel on foot. When provisions were low and game was scarce, some became desperate and ate one of their horses or mules.

Farther south Frémont's party met a group of friendly Utes who helped guide them toward a Mormon outpost at Parowan. Ragged, exhausted, and frostbitten, members of the expedition arrived at the settlement in February 1854. From here, some in the party moved westward with Frémont and reached San Francisco in April. Only one man lost his life on this journey.

Frémont never wrote a report of his fifth expedition. The only account we have is found in Solomon Carvalho's memoirs. The more than three hundred daguerreotypes made by the photographer were later lost in a New York City fire. The trip accomplished little, and neither the Union Pacific nor the Central Pacific Railroads used the routes that Frémont and his men had surveyed.

The exploration days of Frémont were now at an end. Although his last two journeys were mere shadows of earlier accomplishments, the man was still popular. To many, his name continued to be a symbol of bravery and courage.

In his later years, Frémont became involved in business and politics.

Chapter Six

Restless Years

After his explorations, Frémont spent time acquiring more land in California and traveling between the East and West Coasts. The discovery of gold on some of his parcels made him a millionaire. He now owned sawmills, mining operations, and other holdings in San Jose, Monterey, and San Francisco. Overseeing these projects and raising money for their smooth operation took most of his energy and attention.

During this time Frémont often spoke out against slavery and his stand attracted the attention of the **abolitionists**. In 1856, the new Republican Party asked

This is a campaign poster for Frémont's presidential run in 1856.

him to be their candidate for the presidency of the United States. He and his family went east to begin campaigning, but were criticized by Senator Benton and others for turning their backs on the Democratic Party. In the end Frémont lost the election to James Buchanan and once again returned to California.

When war broke out between the northern and southern states, President Lincoln appointed Frémont as major general of the western armies. His job was to defeat the Confederate forces in the territory between the Mississippi and the Rockies. Lacking funds and supplies, he and his men suffered several defeats. In response, he placed Missouri under martial law and ordered all slaves freed. Lincoln, fearing this action might prompt the border states to leave the Union, asked Frémont to withdraw his order. He did, but was later relieved of his command. Once more a cloud of controversy surrounded him.

Ghosts of the Past

After the war, the Frémonts moved to a large home in New York and became active in the social life of the city. Frémont, however, again grew restless. He read everything he could about the areas he had once explored and decided to take a train ride westward. Along the way he passed many of the rocky canyons and rivers where he and his expeditions had camped. Thriving towns and cities now stood in place of the forts and trading centers he once knew.

On his return, Frémont was offered the territorial governorship of Arizona and the family moved to the southwest in 1878. However, the new governor's frequent travels to Washington or New York to raise money for various projects soon resulted in criticism of his leadership. In 1881 Frémont resigned and returned to California.

Extravagant living, dishonest partners, and bad investments gradually erased his fortune. The family survived by living on money that Jessie earned writing books and articles. A trip east in 1890 was John Charles' last. On July 13, ill health brought an end to a once exciting and adventurous life.

Frémont had many critics, but he also had many admirers. The scientific community prized the more than one thousand exotic plants, insects, and other animals he had collected during his explorations. Literary men, such as Ralph Waldo Emerson, Walt Whitman, Henry Wadsworth Longfellow, and Hans Christian Anderson, had nothing but praise for him. Thousands of people both at home and abroad enthusiastically read the accounts of his journeys. He had given them a taste of the excitement and beauty of the great American wilderness and, in so doing, had helped to change the face of the nation.

A Call for Support

Harriet Beecher Stowe, author of *Uncle Tom's Cabin,* spoke out in favor of Frémont's Emancipation Proclamation in Missouri and held a dinner in his honor in New York.

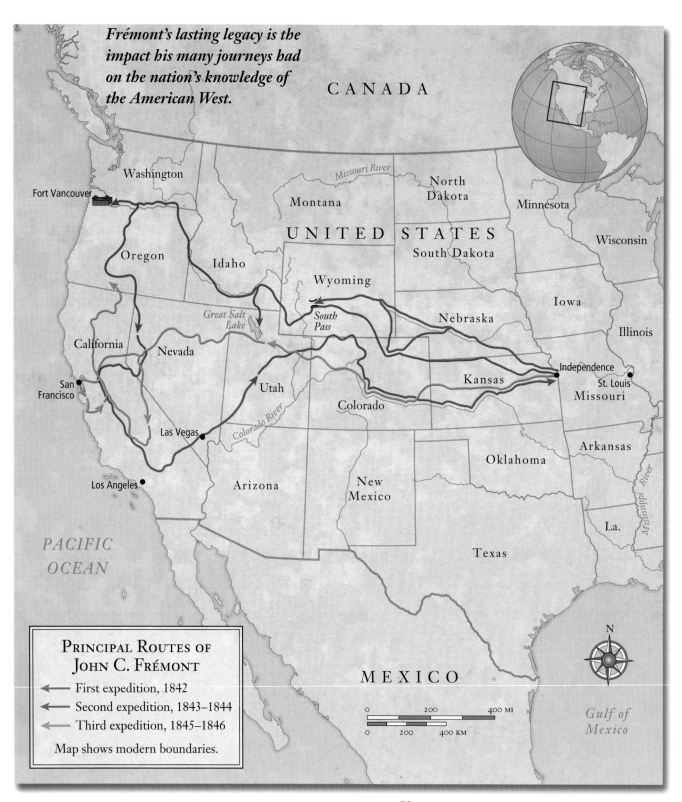

Frémont's lasting legacy is the impact his many journeys had on the nation's knowledge of the American West.

CANADA

UNITED STATES

Washington

Fort Vancouver

Oregon

Idaho

Montana

North Dakota

Minnesota

Wisconsin

South Dakota

Wyoming

Iowa

Missouri River

Great Salt Lake

South Pass

Nebraska

Illinois

California

Nevada

Utah

Colorado River

Colorado

Kansas

Independence

St. Louis

Missouri

San Francisco

Las Vegas

Arizona

New Mexico

Oklahoma

Arkansas

La.

Los Angeles

PACIFIC OCEAN

MEXICO

Texas

Mississippi River

Gulf of Mexico

N

PRINCIPAL ROUTES OF
JOHN C. FRÉMONT

⟵ First expedition, 1842

⟵ Second expedition, 1843–1844

⟵ Third expedition, 1845–1846

Map shows modern boundaries.

0   200   400 MI

0   200   400 KM

Timeline

1813	John Charles Frémont is born in Savannah, Georgia on January 21, to Charles Fremon (later changed to Frémont) of France and Ann Whiting Pryor of Virginia.
1828	Frémont enrolls in Charleston College, South Carolina.
1833	Frémont becomes a mathematics teacher on board the warship, *Natchez*.
1835	Working for the United States Topographical Corps, Frémont helps survey a railroad route from Charleston to Cincinnati.
1836–1837	Frémont surveys Cherokee country with the Topographical Corps.
1837	Frémont accompanies Joseph Nicollet on an expedition into the territory between the Mississippi and Missouri Rivers.
1841	Frémont secretly marries Jessie Benton, daughter of U.S. Senator, Thomas Hart Benton.
1842	Second Lieutenant Frémont leads an expedition to map the Oregon Trail as far as South Pass in Wyoming.
1843–1844	On his second expedition, Frémont reaches Fort Vancouver and then attempts to cross the Rockies during the middle of winter.
1845–1847	During his third expedition, Frémont plays a role in the battle for California and in its surrender.
1848	After being court-martialed for mutiny, Frémont leads a privately funded expedition to survey a western railway route.
1850–1852	Frémont serves as one of first senators from California.

Continued on next page

Timeline *Continued*

1853–1854	Frémont leads a fifth expedition, searching for a central railroad route from St. Louis to California.
1856	Frémont becomes Republican candidate for president of the United States.
1861	During the Civil War, President Lincoln appoints Frémont major general in charge of the Army of the West.
1878–1881	Frémont serves as governor of the Arizona territory.
1890	Frémont dies in New York City on July 13.

Glossary

abolitionist—a person who struggled to end slavery

bartered—traded or exchanged

cartographer—a mapmaker

consul—an official of a government appointed to look after its interests and its citizens in another country

court-martial—to try a member of the armed forces in a military court

daguerrotype—early photographic process or the resulting photograph

emigrant—a person who leaves a country or one part of a country and settles in another

expansionist—a person who favors extending the borders of a country

helmsman—one who steers a boat or ship

hostile—unfriendly or warlike

howitzer—a type of cannon

latitude—the distance, measured in degrees, that is north or south of the equator

longitude—the distance, measured in degrees, that is east or west of Greenwich, England

Manifest Destiny—idea held during the 1800s that the United States was meant to extend its borders from coast to coast

mountain men—trappers and fur traders who explored the American wilderness for adventure or profit

mutiny—refusal to obey a commanding officer

surveyor—one who maps and measures in detail an area of land

transcontinental—across the continent from coast to coast

To Find Out More

Books

Green, Carl R., and William R. Sanford. *John C. Frémont: Soldier and Pathfinder.* New Jersey: Enslow Publishers, 1996.

Harris, Edward. *John Charles Frémont and the Great Western Reconnaissance.* New York: Chelsea House Publishers, 1990.

Hossell, Karen Price. *John C. Frémont.* Portsmouth: Heinemann Library, 2002.

Marcovitz, Hal. *John C. Frémont: Pathfinder of the West.* Philadelphia: Chelsea House Publishers, 2002.

Jaffe, Elizabeth Dana. *The Oregon Trail.* Minnetonka: Capstone Press, 2002.

Sanford, William R., and Carl R. Green. *Kit Carson: Frontier Scout*. New Jersey: Enslow Publishers, 1996.

Santella, Andrew. *Mountain Men*. Connecticut: Children's Press, 2003.

Videos and Films

Across the Plains. Films for the Humanities, 1992.

America's Explorers and Pioneers. Library video.com, 1999.

Pioneer Spirit: Wagon Trains and the Oregon Trail. Rainbow, 2001.

The American Frontier. Schlessinger Media, 2000.

Through the Rockies. Films for the Humanities, 1992.

Organizations and Online Sites

California Historical Society
678 Mission St.
San Francisco, CA 94105
http://www.californiahistoricalsociety.org/
This organization has a collection of primary and secondary sources relating to the history of Frémont in California.

58

California State Military Museum
1119 Second St.
Sacramento, CA 95814
http://www.militarymuseum.org/fremont.html
This museum is a research center devoted to the military history of California. Frémont's role in the California Bear Flag revolt is detailed.

John C. Frémont
http://www.longcamp.com
Articles, images and links to other sites on the explorer can be found here. Information is frequently updated.

Museum Association of Taos
Taos Plaza
Kit Carson Road
Taos, New Mexico 87571
http://www.taoshistoricmuseums.com
Part of the Kit Carson's home, which he purchased for his bride in 1843, reveals facts about the mountain man, his life, and his family, and contains many personal items belonging to them.

Mountain Men
http://xroads.virginia.edu/~HYPER/HNS/Mtmen/home.html
The lives of various fur traders, explorers, and guides are highlighted in articles. Maps and bibliographies are also included.

A Note on Sources

Before writing about Frémont, the explorer, I first read many of his journals, letters, notes, as well as the writings of those who knew him, or accompanied him on one or more of his expeditions. These original documents, found in the Bancroft Library at the University of California, Berkeley, and at the California Historical Society in San Francisco, revealed important clues about the man. Next, I reviewed three volumes at the public library detailing his career, which were: *Travels from 1838-1844*, *The Bear Flag Revolt and Court-Martial*, and *Travels from 1848-1854*, all edited by Donald Jackson and Mary Lee Spence.

Two other volumes gave glimpses of his personal life: *Letters of Jessie Benton Frémont*, edited by Pamela Herr and Mary Lee Spence and *John Charles Frémont: Character as Destiny*, by Andrew Rolle.

—*D. M. Souza*

Index

Numbers in *italics* indicate illustrations.

About the Author

After teaching in both middle grades and high school for several years, D. M. Souza began freelance writing. She has written more than two dozen books for young people including seven for Franklin Watts, including a Watts Library title on another important explorer, *John Wesley Powell*. In her free time, Souza enjoys exploring wilderness areas and observing wild animals. One of the high points in writing about explorers, she admits, was visiting some of the sites they made famous in and around the western United States.